FINISHING LINE PRESS

www.finishinglinepress.com

Moonful

poems by

BeeLyn Naihiwet

Finishing Line Press
Georgetown, Kentucky

Moonful

ACKNOWLEDGMENTS

The following poems have been published in *Uncensored and Unfiltered*, 2024 African-American Writers' Alliance Anthology:

"Black Witness"
"To the Girl Lying Awake Yet Again at 4 AM"
"No Such Thing as Strangers"
"To My Sisters"
"Phases"
"After the Protest"
"Mother Waits for a Better Day"

Publisher: Leah Huete de Maines
Editor: Christen Kincaid
Cover Art: Goitoom Gebru, Instagram account: @gogollage_
Author Photo: Axum Araya
Cover Design: Elizabeth Maines McCleavy

Order online: www.finishinglinepress.com
also available on amazon.com

Author inquiries and mail orders:
Finishing Line Press
PO Box 1626
Georgetown, Kentucky 40324
USA

Table of Contents

For my daughter Mizaan who is the moon,

*And for the tenacious people of Tigray
whose will is ever greater than the odds.*

"It is not unusual to sift through ashes and find an unburnt picture."

—Nikki Giovanni, "The Women Gather"

The Writing on the Wall

I'm a wall defending against
inconvenience and conscience.
I'm the designated witness
to damned courage and deafening
cries. I'm made strong
to withstand wars
on both sides. I'm a wall
against a wall,
against my will.

Black Witness

Exit the bus tunnel through the stairs leading up to 3rd & Pine. Hear the sound of torture, seizing your attention. Look ahead. Spot the two white officers. Watch them brutalize a young Black man on the sidewalk.

See him face down, arms in handcuffs behind his back and legs tied. Hear him yell for them to stop. Hear him scream that it hurts. Hear him beg onlookers to call 911.

See two older Black men stop. Hear them object to an officer who claims that the man is being restricted for his own safety and that of the public. Hear one say, "You don't need to tie him by the legs like that. He's not an animal." Watch as the officer reports that the man tried to kick out the windows in the back of the car. Watch another officer head over to assist.

Walk over and stand next to the Black men. Careful they don't see you see their pain. Hear them try again, "He's in pain. It's excessive force." Hear no response. Say, "Can you imagine them doing that to a white man?" Hear one of them say, "We gotta get going." Move to let them pass.

Hear a voice from behind, "No, I can't imagine that." Turn to spot the young white man, standing against the wall of the McDonald's. Watch more police cars and an ambulance arrive. Look as passersby pause before going their way.

See the still-living Black man writhe in pain. Hear him continue to wail. Stay and see, and never stop seeing.

To the Girl Lying Awake Yet Again at 4 AM

I don't know how to keep things alive, you say
when asked why you're lonely, although
the truth is that you love like it's a house
and move in with all your longings.
Perhaps you could try visiting instead
and haul only your attention along. Hold it
close if possible. Practice being more
wise than willing, more human
than hoping, more known than needed,
more free than favored, more person
than pawn. Accept death and life equally.
Fully expect that you'll break apart.

Fork

I think ruin is the most beautiful word;
sudden, the most cruel.
I feel like only the moon
truly understands.
There's no right or wrong way
to respond to violence.
I know you can love someone
into unloving you.

What is Home When it Turns on You?

What is home when it turns on you?
Is it still home? Was it ever home?
You know now that home is
where the hate is, where the heart
knows no peace and so it goes,
falling to pieces.

Try to keep it together as you run
for cover, as you rush to gather
essentials for your escape. Go
and keep going. And dare
to look back at the devastation.
Be still and remember that dust
is the source of life.

How We Kill

Grandma calls my youngest sister
"The Middle One." I remind her
of the birth order. She dismisses me
with a flick of the wrist and says,
I know that, but she's in between
the beautiful one and the black one.

Dear Sleep

It's not that I'm bitter as much
as that I'm better off without you.
You sneak up silently behind me
and cover my eyes with your heavy hands.
I slide out of your overbearing embrace
like those of my dad's friends growing up.
You whisper for me to relax, let go.
No. I have calls to make.

Back home my grandmother is just waking up,
soon to walk all those miles
to church in the white Converses
I took for her on my last visit.

You follow me to the window. I turn my back
to you. You don't respect my boundaries,
ignore my request for space,
show up unannounced. You insist
on being useful in spite
of myself. I resist.

You remind me of a shifty salesman
playing both sides, promising rest
that cheats death—"The Best Around!"
Your record speaks for itself.
Unlike my mother.

To you, her death was within an acceptable
margin of error. To me, it led to a lifetime
of skepticism toward anything that requires
my trust without earning it.
I'm tired. No, I don't want to lie down.

We can't go on like this.

Sometimes you find me on the couch
in the middle of the night, hold me
as if you're sorry,

as if you mean it,
as if you wish you could bring
back my mother.

Just Enough

Some doors are better left unopened,
but you've always been the curious type,
which is to say, you've been dissatisfied
for so long. *I'm tired of getting my hopes up,*
you write to whomever will read your journals
when you're gone. You spend your life
with its end in hand. Every door is a chance at
a journey so great its destination is unknown.
You approach with a history of knowing
just enough to survive.

Tigray

I dream of returning to you next time to stay,
and reclaiming what was lost when I first fled.

I dream of who I might've been holding hands
with who I've become, inspired and in solidarity.

I dream of the spirit of my mother, long buried,
rising in recognition and impossible reunion.

I dream of chasing my brothers, gathering
and keeping them safe, whole and alive.

I dream of climbing to Grandma's roof
to get a closer look at God.

I dream of us, blessed and brave.
I dream of us, festive and free.

I dream and dare
expect.

In the Kitchen

The women joke about men who left: "I'll get a new one before you do."
"If you do, we'll have to share." Laughter. They tease each other about
the man-who-left details. "Oh, yours was just silly." "What's worse, silly
or cruel?" More laughter. They tell me to look for the right things in a
partner. Someone who loves you like a sister, they say. I hear, someone
who will stay.

Hayal: ሐያል

Growing up they called me ሐያል—difficult. Even before I understood all the connotations I knew it was disapproval. This word was readily thrown at me by family and members of the community whenever I questioned or objected to forms of inequality—sexism, misogyny, gender roles, and general double standards. Men and women warned that I would never get married unless I learned to accept the way things are. I remember feeling relieved that I might inadvertently escape marriage, a fate that seemed not unlike prison to me. Marriage did not elude me, though I would swiftly save myself from an ill-fitting one. What continues to be out of reach is a world that values girls, women, and persons apart from our proximity to men or patriarchal values. All the same, this ሐያል remains hopeful and committed to the effort. In the words of Arundhati Roy: *Another world is not only possible, she's on her way. On a quiet day, I can hear her breathing.*

Ever the Revolution

You are what greatness
looks like in black skin.

No greater act than remaining whole
in spite of every shattering thing.

They fear your skin deep, ever
the revolution, brilliant in the dark.

Death is Also Ours

"When it's raining out, does it not fall on everyone equally?" My father treats my grieving heart with rationale. It's unhelpful, mostly because I'm guilty of feeling grief harder when it visits my family. He speculates that the person who told him the news of his nephew's murder withheld the death of his sister. "He couldn't bring himself to tell me that my sister is also dead." I keep crying. He continues to name other members of our family who were likely home when soldiers raided and killed Ma'Asho. He's preparing himself, bracing for more loss. Images of my cousin's tender smile and listening eyes flash across my mind, his gentleness in stark contrast to the gore of war. Lying on the ground, lifeless. I struggle to breathe. My father softens, "እጆኪ, my daughter. The only thing we can do is accept it." Therein lies my problem. I think of Grandma, who was confused by my reaction on one of my visits to the town crier's wailing nearly every morning. "It's the most heartbreaking sound. How are people supposed to live when they're greeted with death morning after morning?" I said. She replied, "አይትዓሸዊ. Is there living without death? Death is also ours." I tried to make a stronger case for life, but lost to my own desperation. I think now, *How do I accept that my beloved Ma'Asho is dead? How do I accept that this life that I love continues to take from me people I love? How do I accept the unacceptable?*

After

To lose is to find forever.
End to begin.
Leave to un-last
your breath and stay.

Mother

I glimpsed you this afternoon in your granddaughter
as she and I played a game of hide-and-seek.
She hasn't yet caught on to the disconnect between
the concept of the game and her habitual hiding place.
I called out her name and noisily pretended
to search under a pillow, on the bookshelf,
inside the dresser, before approaching
the closet in which she would surely be.
Suddenly I feared that she'd slipped out
and may have fallen down the stairs.
I burst into the closet in a panic.
She giggled with sheer delight
and exclaimed, "I found you!"
Beloved, I'm always where
I'm looking for you.

For the First Time

He apologizes to her.
Her eyes mark the date and time,
memorialize the moment.
She has and hasn't been waiting
for this never of humility.
Maybe he does love her.
This love, had she missed it? Had he?
"I'm sorry for making you angry. I hope
you can forgive me, please." He now says
what she has said to him for years.
The dictator of her life bows
to her at last and this is how
she loses him.

Homework

I'm doing the dishes as Mama who's mine and not mine tells me about a hard conversation with a friend of hers. I stop when it hits me that she's asking for advice. The ceiling lowers. I ache for open sky. What would you tell me, I say. You're the one with education, she says, and looks away. I hate everything. I don't have words for the way I feel. I tell her that school taught me that the most important lessons are learned at home. She laughs shyly, starts drying the dishes. When she continues her story, I listen with all my might.

Big Boy on the Brink

Six foot three at twenty-one years old,
your long, looming, hormonal, awkward
run-on of a frame stands out.
Mama shares you'd stayed up all night playing
video games and offers me coffee like an apology.

I call out to you as I try to find the least blurry TV channel.
I hear you grunting as you roll your heaviness
out of your dungeon of a bedroom.
Your towering head and stooped shoulders enter
the living room first, dragging your never-ending legs.

Your dreadlocks-to-be are ambivalent
about making a home of your head, as if they've overheard
your absurd alignment with All Lives Matter.
You drop full length on the couch, legs dangling.
The recent arm tattoo of Mama's name is now exposed.

It's not that deep, you balked when I once commented.
I study the image now, no pressure to downplay or collude
with your denial of attachment to your story
and Mama who kept and raised you at all costs:
a father who refused to stay and stayed gone,
and the hard road of poor, Black motherhood.

I say I stopped by because I'd missed you.
You scoff. You have twenty-one years of practice
that you don't care to be missed,
to be seen, to be wanted.
You turn your face away again.
But not before I catch your eyes—
a troubled sea on the brink of a flood.

Go Gently

Go to the depth of your grief
and stay only as long
as you can.

Be gentle with yourself:
There's a hole in the heart
of a heart in a hole.

After the Protest

I hang the Tigray flag back on my bedroom wall. In the middle of the
night when my baby stirs in her crib, I rub her head until she falls asleep.
Her nightlight gives the room a reddish glow, turning the red on the flag
into blood, the yellow of its star into brown skin. I stand between two
worlds—bloodshed on one side, budding life on the other. I return to bed
as details clash in my mind: My little brother back home riding his bike
to a neighbor's to ask for food, my coffee date plans with a friend in the
morning, noting Day 618 of the Tigray Genocide, anxiety about not getting
enough sleep to take optimal care of my baby. The wind enters through the
window. The flag waves in the dark. I tell myself it's not goodbye.

Raising Standards

If you're a girl who's raised as a boy
you grow up believing that your voice matters
that you can make statements instead of suggestions
that learning to cook is optional, unnecessary
that your looks are an afterthought, if they're thought of at all
that inconvenience is infrequent
that permission is to be granted, not only asked for
that you're at the mercy of your own shortcomings, not that of others
that the work you do is recognized, not overlooked
And you would survive
if it were a different world

Moonbound

When men waste your heart
You become the woman
Of your dreams and fly

You learned early on
That roots splinter and break
The sky, edgeless touch

Free in sun and storm
You soar above a man's world
Transcending limits

A no to downfall

Heir

As a kid I asked my mother
if it hurt to see my father
with his new family.

She said it helped.

The Light is Greater

for Tigray

They came along to convince you
that you didn't matter.
It was their shame that gripped you, listing
everything that broke in your possession—
pure evil acting out perverse justice.
Did the darkness grow easier to bear
than the curious light ahead?
Consider that the light is your reflection.
Don't you know that not everything
that breaks, breaks away?
You're greater than what they did to you.
This world is a friend to no one.
It would have you believe all is lost.
Don't you know that the level of struggle
is equal to the power you hold?
They came with their worst.
But it was you who withstood
and remained
faithful.

What They Don't Tell You

It's possible to end up with more goodbyes than people.
Some people come in the name of fun and leave a funeral in their wake.
Desire is quicksand. Be quicker.

Flowers Know My Name

The woman who represents every wrong
and evil thing that ever happened to me
happens to be named Abeba—*flower.*
This detail has disturbed me for many years.
I still don't know how to reconcile the meaning
of her name with her self-serving use
of my past traumas against me.
People tell me to let it go, but the past objects
to its name and even the dead get flowers.
She has followed me into every significant moment,
claiming membership by name alone.
If only she'd been named something more fitting,
like a bomb, a snake, a disease.
Lately I've wondered if this isn't God's glory—
the juxtaposition of good and evil, charging me
to ensure that goodness triumphs.
Embattled, I'm becoming
what I love and flowers
know my name.

When Heartbreak Comes

When heartbreak comes, greet her warmly
and let her in. Offer her a cool glass of water
and orient her to the lay of your heart: *You can
stay as long as you need. Many women live here,
lovers and warriors all. They will be your guides.*

Moonful

Racing heart leaps to
override caution, wrapping
itself in your name.

It gathers your face
and dear words, nestling in sound
possibilities.

The moon draws nearer,
full of longing for the heart
to praise moonlight again.

Fall, unfold the night.

What Happens to Love

What happens to love
between those on opposite sides of a war?
It gets caught in the crossfire, bleeding
out in the street, barely breathing
long enough to say,
So this is us—dying
to win.

No Such Thing as Strangers

Gio, the Lyft driver, pulls up to the front of the brunch spot and gets out to help me with my luggage. I'm very touched even though I know it's standard customer service, just as I'd fought back tears when the waiter told me to take my time in spite of the line that had started to form at the door. Everything hurts lately and any kind gesture becomes God. Gio asks if I mind country music and I say I prefer it; it suits my melancholy. I tell him this had been a business trip, which is only partly true. He wishes me success with my book. We talk about places we've lived, belonging and lack thereof. Gio tells me that he was closest to his grandmother who passed away a few years ago, how losing her changed him; that he's now intentional about living every moment of his life to the fullest; about finding the beauty in every interaction, every circumstance—no matter what, he says. He tells me that his grandmother used to say that there is no such thing as strangers. I don't mention my beloved late grandmother whom I miss with the weight of all tomorrows. I say, Sounds like your grandmother was a wonderful person. She is, Gio replies, she really is. There was no stopping the tears. I keep my head down so he wouldn't see me fall apart. We ride Luke Comb's "Better Together" in silence. I tell him to take his time because I have three hours before my flight takes off. He asks if there were any more places I wanted to check out before leaving the city. Not really, I say, before recalling an Instagram post that day about a protest in town against the Tigray Genocide. I tell him about the six-month-long war, the communications blackout, the starvation, the rape, the 150,000 deaths, and the world's indifference to the plight of my people. I look out the window as I talk, tears streaming down my face. Sometimes, I say, I don't know if my heart is hardening or away. He falls silent, then says solemnly, I can't believe I haven't heard anything about this. He asks me to look up the details of the protest and says he'll take me, adding, I'll park the car and go with you; you don't have to do this alone. We drive to the location and search in several directions, but can't find the protesters. It turns out the protest ended an hour earlier. I'm disappointed, but feel better for his generous spirit. Gio says he'll take the scenic route to the airport and points out beautiful art and architecture along the way. I sit up, captivated by various colors and shapes. I think about our grandmothers, his and mine, their everlasting love guiding us home.

The Case for Ghosts

The survivor defeated shame
and lived to tell.
The listeners feared scandal
and denied it.

It takes a village
to bury a crime.

Love, Fluently

On my last birthday before motherhood
I slip into my late mother's dress.
I gaze into the full-length mirror
where my round belly protrudes
and summon my mother's arms
to wrap around me. My daughter
kicks and her hand rises to my stomach
in a language that says, *I'm here.*
How do I gift my daughter her grandmother
who is gone but never left me?
I slip into my mother's dress,
a language I speak.

To My Sisters

Black woman, I know you're tired.
You've long held up the sky.
Rest your arms, my dear;
they belong at your sides.

May they plummet and burn
this land of hate.
Let this inferno rage and claim
every brutal plot and deed,
sparing no potential threat.

You are everything
you need to survive a firestorm—
a blessed body of water, rising
to swallow it whole.

Worldview

There has to be a way,
says the world.

There is,
the moon replies.

How?

Stop turning
away.

History is a Woman

for Monaliza Abraha

You wade through the torrent, learning
your own depths, surprising only
yourself. You've survived
many storms—swallowing shock,
suspending sound, sinking
stones, and struck
when you glimpse God
within.

On Becoming Mizaan's Mother

Moon Eyes, you make me
forget everything but you
You create me so

Tell me the story
about you and the angels
How I became home

You have made me rich
What is money to a moon
full of tenderness

I want for nothing

Give Yourself a New Name

Who are you without your past?
What if you decided right now to live
like you'd never seen the inside
of the world's mouth? Say you will
do it—give yourself a new name.
Grow a garden. Make glory of it.
Then create your God.

Terminal

Over-valuing others.
Giving blind loyalty to your fears.
Being an accomplice to your own victimization.
Not taking yourself seriously.
Seeing with your feelings.
Surviving your life.

Things I'll Tell My Daughter

Love is what happens when you're waiting for love.
Authenticity may be the lonelier road, but it's the most fortified.
The strongest man is a feminist.
There are those whose hearts are open, though their tongues are tied.
Friendly fire is fire.
Learning acceptance includes your gifts.
You can't kill love, but you can kill its chances.
Respecting yourself reveals the other person.
There is a kind of struggle that is power.
The right question is often the answer.
Your blessings are people-proof.
Unjourneyed love is hollow love.
If there must be brokenness, negotiate for beauty.
It's smart not to burn bridges; it's wise to let some burn.
There's no such thing as a sweet wolf.
Desire can travel across a burnt bridge without needing to be met.
There comes a time when quitting is winning.
It may be a man's world, but the expert witness is a woman.
Courage is never wasted.
There's a lot to be said for closeness, but distance has the fuller view.
God is in every outcome.
Holding on to yourself is a superpower.

Packing

He's the reassuring type,
declares I'll-never-leave type.
He's the controlling type,
neglects permission-to-stay type.

She's the feminist type,
declares human-before-woman type.
She's the critical type,
neglects hurt-in-him type.

Two sides of baggage.

Tree of Truth

Your new eyes reveal the rot
of the garden you cultivated
from debris.

Dig deeper.

Sometimes you have to
hit rock bottom
to grow roots.

When Water Boils

You turn away from me
in search of burning flame.
I am the sea.

I drift by gently, careful
not to cross the shoreline.

You spot the fire.
Sparks fly as you
meet your match.

I wave to you,
but you're mesmerized.

You swelter in the heat
until you're engulfed,
burning.

Only the fire
waves.

Breaking News

Someone should've told you
that betraying yourself is no defense
against devastation by others.
You broke your own heart as if
you'd be safer in pieces, as if
you could snap out of it, as if
you would crack some code.
How could you've known that
it's harder to forgive yourself
than to reconstruct a heart.

The Work of a Woman

for Axumawit

It's insufficient to write a poem
for a poem, but these wanting words
are prepared to pale.

Axumawit, aptly named, you
stand tall against wicked attacks
that have toppled others.

I testify to the light you wrested
from the darkness, to the water
you became in drought.

You've grown love—
the work of a woman,
a world of example.

Praise

He came to her like
an answered prayer and so,
evidence of God.

The full form of him
she leapt to touch and revel
in true homecoming.

A flower boy turned
garden turned moon of a man,
faithful in the dark.

The answer was no.

When Your Family in Tigray is Trapped in a War

You see war everywhere
between the couple at the café
in traffic on the freeway
among children on the playground
in line at the bank
between strangers on the sidewalk
on the basketball court
among friends at the bar
in online comments
in the weather
in the mirror

Precedent

Because you said my hand felt like flowers.
Because you said I looked like God.
Because you said you'd love me until the stars drown.
Because you said my love meant that you were alive.
Because you said I was the bow to your strings.
Because you said we were a match made in heaven.
Because we didn't make it here on earth.

Wheel of Forsaken

Some people leave
for the same reason
they came.

Others return
for the same reason
they left.

They run
in circles.

I Swear

for WeyNalem

In another world we are children
of worth, not war
There are no drills
in preparation for bad men
who barge into homes
to kill young men
and violate women and girls
You're not frozen with terror
and I'm not pretending
to be brave
In another world we're quick to laughter
and play without fear
of crossfire
We don't flee in the moonlight
Silence, a necessity so severe
it becomes a sentence
We grow into softness,
not survivors who are their scars
and secrets
In another world our mother lives
to old age and we are not ghosts
chasing after her memory
We remain human
and don't suffer a psychotic break
from encounters
with repressed details
The faces of our childhood friends
are not sunken
from languishing in poverty
In another world you don't mistake
a bottle for our mother
until it shatters into decades
of addiction and danger
I don't make a mother
out of her absence and fall
in love with everything that is lost
In another world we are children

Phases

Green, like loving a thing so much you can't stand it.
Loud, like the elephant in the room.
Edgy, like nearly losing your mind.
Layers, like there's this you and that you and they keep in touch.
Short, like giving notice.
Backwards, like self-sabotage.
Mismatch, like sorry and repeat.
Warm, like getting closer to the answer.
Formal, like it's personal.
Black, like the blueprint.
Casual, like God's timing.
Identical, like fear and hate.
Fancy, like an open mind.
Trendy, like learning the hard way.
Smart, like getting away with it.
Playful, like there's no yesterday.
Sheer, like speaking your heart.
Comfortable, like upheld boundaries.
Vintage, like redemption.
Timeless, like it's the last time.
Simple, like there's no other choice.
Classic, like denial.
Artsy, like self-consciousness.

Things Later Regretted

after Sei Shōnagan

Letting your loneliness make the decision to
become more than friends. Taking the high
road to avoid being fully human. Convincing
yourself that what he does is separate from
who he is. Accepting being chosen instead of
doing the choosing. Neglecting the suffering of
women who undermine your liberation.
Confusing your standards for baggage.
Playing small. Paying big.

A Guy Walks into a Poem

Him: Hey, wanna take me downtown? I'm meeting some people.

Her: No, I will not be doing anything for anyone today.

Him: What? That's a thing?

Her: Yeah. In fact, it's your thing.

Him: Who wakes up and say, "I will not be doing anything for anyone today"?

Her: You don't have to say it when you live it.

Him: You could just not say it.

Her: I actually have to say it. Just like we have to say "Black Lives Matter" even though we shouldn't have to. We have to say things to people whose way of life makes us have to say it.

Him: Yeah, that makes sense.

Her: See, that's one thing I did for you today.

500 Days of Tigray Genocide

My heart is a world.
In it Tigray is free.
The land neither besieged
nor looted. The air clear
of strikes and slaughter.
Our bodies no longer
battlefields. Our love
the only thing
burning.

The Sequel

I'm in the front seat as you drive down Rainier Ave.
It's 2:30 AM. I surprised us both when I agreed to
go to wherever it is we're going—*the homie got
an after-hours spot.* I'd intended to go home after
the bar closed, but some restlessness gripped me
and there you were in your blue flannel shirt over
a white tee buttoned only at the neck like a cape,
a walking throwback to the adventures of my
youth. Sure enough, I agreed to a feeling.
You play West Coast gangsta rap so loud you don't
hear my objection until I turn it down and suggest
something a little more friendly. You laugh and
tease, I see you're trying to set the mood. Kinda.
I'm trying to rewrite the story. We arrive to find
the spot closed and sit in the parking lot as you
make calls trying to keep the night young. I narrate
the scene to my best friend over text, who's amused
by my impromptu trip down memory lane. Neither
she nor I is surprised when it leads to a dead end.

Reap

He created a monster
and called it love.
The monster found love
and turned on him.

Symptoms of a Life Almost Lived May Include

You've always known what you don't want
Fear those you love
Still become everything you feel
Did not say no all those years
Can't trust yourself to give up
There is no one safe enough to tell
You hide in plain sight
Worship words
You can never decide if you're bad or good
Have difficulty with accepting the unknown
Feel guilt about wanting to be loved the way you love
Mistake the beginning for the end

Barely

Let's say the war ends
and we remember
ourselves
before strange times
made us strangers

Farewellcome

We embrace and weep
Beloved, there's no warning
for what's ahead
Let's say we believe
that barely
is survival still

Driving Lessons

Where did we go wrong
or were we ever right?
You're a fading memory
that was once so here.
You couldn't leave alone.
The moon followed right behind you.
Only your promises linger,
unkept. Did you ever mean any of it?
The silence is answer enough.
Our love was a one-way street.
I was headed the wrong way.

Mother Waits for a Better Day

for the mothers of Tigray

Mother waits because better is a child
Who knows the way home
She blesses delay
And banishes despair
                    ሰላም መንገዲ።

Mother wrestles with God
Refuses to forfeit her children
She pulls strength from the earth
Mother to mother

Mother waits because better is a child
Who raises the village
She knows glory belongs
To the grassroots
                    ክብረት ይሃበልና።

Mother wounds with her love
Fierce and heart-striking
She confronts the fire
And makes it weep

Mother waits because better is a child
Whose victory is a birthright
She creates a shield of mothers
A defense force of life
                    ብሓደ ከም ሓደ።

Parallel

His love turned
into a discreet river that
channels her.

Her love turned
into a faint moon that
reflects him.

Dear One

It's far too easy to deny yourself
the very thing you desire, and so it is
with me. I've been trying to return to us
for a couple of months. For what
it's worth I think I understand the obstacle
better now. Return is a deceptive word.
It doesn't address the nevermore. You return
to an end that makes a beginner of you.

The Word Was Us

We were walking back to your place after dinner
when an unruly thunderstorm hit. I just knew
the world was ending. There was no other explanation
for the torrential assault that made it difficult to breathe.
I clung to you. I remembered how I'd once said
I wanted to be in love when the worst happened.
Everything around us shook and people ran in all directions.
You wrapped your arms around me, said that thunderstorms
were common in the area. Don't fear, you added.
I cried and ranted that the pandemic was God's
rebuke, the thunderstorm surely his wrath.
We found shelter under the awning of a restaurant.
You drew me closer, your heart beating in my ears.
You fear your God is punishing you, you said
as you pulled out your phone and held it in front of my face.
On the wet screen I read your God's words
and felt calm. The future arrived then.

Taste of Color

A mouth is just a mouth until
it becomes a well. Desire,
what depth you have.
I dive from the world, wade
in the dark. Taste
the afterlife.

Love me in color.
Say I'm yours in red
and yellow. Show me
the brave in your blood,
the bouquet of your breath.

Love me in Tigray.

A Moon is Born

for my daughter Mizaan

You arrived and immediately absolved
all who'd broken my heart.
Their unintended benevolence emerged,
illuminated in your light.
Every tear I ever shed rose and returned.
Sleepless nights sighed in relief and redemption.
Pages of heartache clamored and clapped.
Lost time flew and found me.
Unanswered questions took a bow.
Closed doors stood in ovation.
Unkept promises turned into promotion.
My story revealed itself as written.
My life ran up ahead, announcing,
I've swallowed the night. If you're looking
for the moon, she'll be with me.

Moonside

There is no question
Of lives that matter on the moon
Illuminating

The beauty of night
Deeply moving example
I gladly follow

Freedom is moonside
Full embrace of vast Blackness
Makes my world go round

There is no stopping

Coloring Outside the Lines

My friend asks if the color of the heart
emoji matters. I say it seems so.
He describes inconsistent use in text exchanges
across genders, moods and contexts.
I tell him I use whatever color I feel like, though
there's no telling how it's interpreted by recipients.
He decides to avoid heart emojis altogether: "Better safe than weird."
"Or you could use the black one," I say. "Can't go wrong
with Black love."

With is the Greatest Word

Every day finds me
an ever first time, noting
the wild fact of you

Whom is whose is whom
Longing compelled destiny
A definite yes

A moment expands
A heart beats outside a body
A reason enters

Everything changes

Surviving Genocide

When the days are dark
and you're broken and bound,
you twist and turn in pain
And you turn and turn
And you turn into tomorrow

Bright is the light within you,
besting death,
birthing a dream

I watch as you lift your arms
And bring down the heavens

Your life is a great deed

The Way Beauty Saves

The world says, You're too soft,
only the strong survive
between a rock and a hard place.
I say, Is that a dare?

The author (left) with her older sister, WeyNalem before leaving Tigray, Ethiopia as refugees in the 80s.

BeeLyn Naihiwet is a Seattle-based Black poet from Tigray. She is passionate about her work as a mental health therapist, social justice, motherhood, and the moon. *Moonful* is her second book of poetry. Her debut poetry collection, *Plenty,* was published by Finishing Line Press in 2021.

Milton Keynes UK
Ingram Content Group UK Ltd.
UKHW030637191124
451300UK00006B/137

9 798888 387979